salmonpoetry

Publishing Irish & International

Poetry Since 1981

Stichomythia n. /stɪkəʊˈmɪθɪə/ **Etymology:** modern Latin Greek στιχομῦθία, στίχος STICHOS n. + μῦθος speech, talk. In classical Greek Drama, dialogue in alternate lines, employed in sharp disputation, and characterized by antithesis and rhetorical repetition or taking up of the opponent's words. Also applied to modern imitations of this.

—*Oxford English Dictionary* (2016)

Stichomythia
TYLER FARRELL

Published in 2018 by
Salmon Poetry
Cliffs of Moher, County Clare, Ireland
Website: www.salmonpoetry.com
Email: info@salmonpoetry.com

ISBN 978-1-912561-01-8

COVER ARTWORK: *The Burren* by Douglas Koepsel
COVER DESIGN & TYPESETTING: *Siobhán Hutson*

Printed in Ireland by Sprint Print

For: Joan (for her strength), Holden, Linus,
Cynthia, Jim and my brother, Brian.

My special thanks to fellow poet and teacher,
Jenna Green Azab whose adventurous spirit,
editorial expertise, and eternal friendship I am grateful for.

Also, this book is dedicated to the memory of
poet James Liddy, and artist Liam O'Connor

Acknowledgments

Thanks are due to the editors of the following in which some of these poems have previously appeared: *Burdock, Burning Bush 2, The Blue Canary, Poetry Speaks* (Madison Museum of Contemporary Art), *Wisconsin Fellowship of Poets, The Marquette University Literary Review, Presence: A Journal of Catholic Poetry, Solitary Plover, Eat Local :: Read Local, Verse Wisconsin, The Proper Mustard, St. Peter's B-List: Contemporary Poems Inspired by the Saints* (edited by Mary Ann B. Miller) and *Even the Daybreak: 35 Years of Salmon Poetry* (edited by Jessie Lendennie).

Using up their last heat our hearts
Will be two huge candles
Reflecting their double light
In both our minds
Twin
Mirrors.

    —CHARLES BAUDELAIRE
     "The Death of Lovers" CXXI
     Translated by James Liddy (1975)

*

Scratch an Irish poet, and if the scratch is deep enough
to draw blood, the result, however heretical it may be,
will be a religious poem.

    —HORACE GREGORY
     from "The Dying Gladiators
     of Samuel Beckett" (1956)

Contents

I
Ou j'oublie tout de suite ou je n'oublie jamais

II
Letters to James

III
Ephemeral

IV
Je suis comme ça

I

Ou j'oublie tout de suite ou je n'oublie jamais

—SAMUEL BECKETT, *Waiting for Godot*

Both then were silent?

Silent, each contemplating the other in both mirrors of the reciprocal flesh of theirhisnothis fellowfaces.

—JAMES JOYCE, *Ulysses*
Episode 17: Ithaca

Bar Time Haze, Stray Thoughts

Mirror makers know the secret – one does not make a mirror
to resemble a person, one brings the person to a mirror.

—JACK SPICER, *"Dear Joe" (1958)*

Large Old Style mirror
wall of Riverwest, Milwaukee
tavern. I remain hidden, my flaws, my ideas.
Mirrors tell me something inverted
opposite lightness behind the bar
reflections of society members
boys and girls laughing large glasses
overturned on tables. No one thinks about
tomorrow, grand bargains the great beyond
missteps into angled directions. Give up
whiskey next week, next month the nightmares
and the bulk of life. Start walking more
ways to outside for another cigarette on
the avenue earth. Ladders into the sky
we want to feel good about ourselves.
I can see, hear them clearer now, loudness
increasing the dirty walls, the door opens
suddenly wind overtakes our spirits
sweeps thru the darkened room, away from
the mirror, away from this place.
People themselves never remember
who they were, are, want to be. The mirror
never itself either. Mirrors shift, reflect
distort hide and advertise. Kingdoms
point to humankind. Customary ways in which
young women saw visions, old men dreamed dreams.
Never myself I am one of them. Like the mirror
we promote, confess to the night outside
or to no one. People listen to bar noise
ignore the mirror, my eyes in the mirror
my face reflecting the lights suddenly turned on
people shuffling toward the exit
end of the evening, begin lives the final night
which way to live, questions inseparable.
We are closer now than breathing.

The Cathedral/Basilica of Saint Louis, King of France

Christ, we drank.

—JAMES LIDDY, *"The Quarter"*

If we could live in this parish forever
we could be truly happy our entire lives.

Then a wedding opens chilled cathedral doors
with smells of an ordination at the Vatican.
Grey marble and incense – intoxicates
honors the crowd, union heat throb Christ.
Sounds draw us nearer the ground in reverence
kneeling beneath the sun and crescent moon.
Our minds now unclouded, sins confessed.
Forgiveness is a city of saints, Louis singing
a song for Saint Joseph. He sings also
for the sinners – Bourbon Street window swingers
bad barkers next to three card monty dealers
near Café Du Monde where a homeless man
hit on me as we sat on black iron benches in the park
with the Civil War cannon, model 1861 parrot rifle.
He said I had real fair skin and I was sweating.
Beignet powdered sugar fell everywhere.
I smiled, listened, chatted with him for a time
about artillery and pirates, about the Jax brewery,
voodoo. Then I went and had a few beers
at the brewery, stumbled back to the Basilica
and with other flaming hearts looked skyward.
We prayed, recited plaque history, visitations
always pondering a pilgrimage to another bar.
Revelation love from local parishioners
indulging the way sinners often indulge.

Three Family Rummage

Signs sang locals up the crest of Hill Cr.
with the deal hungry who looked and sought
what and where did those hubcaps come from
while we sat grandma's lap on the davenport
green for sale the back porch, in and out of kitchens
garage boxes filled with old shirts and coats
toys and useless trinkets, dishes priced at top dollar.
My mother, my aunts tailoring every one time need
counting the money in the box, joy to squelch
the haggler. "Well…I couldn't take anything lower
than twenty dollars for that coat. It's brand new
and the seed company patch is quite unique."

And the kids are looking at the toys and I am
trying on an old shirt of my grandfather's
while the poker face people hit the pavement
with some old junk for a few dollars here and
springs Veronica pushed on an elderly lady
with a walker thinking her neighbor boy could
fix her bed with them. And Father Upanup
out of his classics lurking in the books
ready to ask for them, a donation to the church
perhaps. All the while my aunts holding onto
stuff out of spite. She laughed at the ridiculous offer
of fifty cents for a Monopoly game. And here
I thought the idea of a rummage sale was
to get rid of stuff, to clean house, to unburden.
But, as always, my family would consider
the money angle, greed over clutter. A thought
glory flash of timing and profit, old supply sold
to the poor and the needy, the selfish and greedy.

Poem for Hart Crane

*I don't want to use you as a makeshift when my principle ambition and life lies
completely outside of business…You will perhaps be righteously a little bewildered
at all these statements about my enthusiasm about my writing and my devotion
to that career in life…Be all this as it may, I have come to recognize that I am
satisfied and spiritually healthy only when I am fulfilling myself in that direction.*

——HART CRANE, in a letter to his father — January 12, 1924

As I write, North America knows loss
(as all the world knows loss)
real jobs shackle like creations.
Words let in
sight, the spell of machines
noise line forgotten
sound drowned in rye — brown faint hints
light the acetylene glow.
Father's candy pays bills — son whose life/death
all forgotten
even from new ships helmed by poets.

Mother, let me help with your eyesight
sore, grandmother's estate I see
her friend Billy dance the city swamp
large girders overlook the sun
drenched sea.

I shall think of him in light
apples at the table
overturned bowls in the sink.
Caribbean when I get a chance
never
I won't ask for help —
manual labor letters
let inner fears seethe
Hectic profit with no modesty
spells cannot afford
provincial passages written about tower rooms
settled an education.
This fuses America
powers in sky frosted windowpane.

My relations never seem to comprehend
waters of greed and ideal.

Instructions for a Wisconsin Poetry Center

The satisfactory emphasis is on revolving.

—LORINE NIEDECKER, January 1935

James Liddy led students yearly
preacher/teacher like to Lorine's Rock River.
We followed the ring of flowers flow
catfish and carp seined from Lake Koshkonong
immersed in a flooded season.

James faith dropped students – baptized
with phrases, Niedecker's word world island,
the isolation even for birds. Black Hawk
wells up in us daily. We plunge and fish for
books/letters/poems buried in sand-mud over hills
the marsh cranes sing weather rain music.

Lorine, bird woman, sights verbal mud moons
condensation on pages, authors animated bulrush
stony undersides. Small cabin and bars, of course
she drank grasshoppers at Club 26, stories
of poets, town gravesites painted with quiet solitude.

Gem stones adorn the poet's eyes the surface
of her poems, her life. Shadows of Liddy
living poet into poet into water from branches
cling to and bend down rivers. For it was water
all the time. Dry pages curved from water's use
letters telling tales of natural days and nights.

We dreamt those wooden green art walls
pictured her poor grey gulls, borrowed
words and books from her library.
James instructed with Lorine. We answered
every spring with markings on habitat
tree trunks with high water marks
at a distance like millions of Lorine's ducks
taking off suddenly, a dark wave of embrace.

Fort Atkinson

If you circle the habit of your meaning it's fact and no harm done.

—LORINE NIEDECKER, February 1935

Black Hawk and White Crow
fly high over history. The General
specifically waits for provisions
from Winnebago wagons – haul
over ground on holiday.
Roads to portage and miles of swamp
land they wander deliberate, muster
out eyes from an old rip named wilderness.
Nourishment lacks patience
people fight for land without
new cartographers.

Black Hawk wars fought on the plains,
gullies for mid-western peoples
long dead buried underground
when the land soft without rock
markers or names of wild
animals, trees cut for shelters.
Other bodies blessed in marshes
on pine platforms surveying the horizon
hand of black soot from fires
and mark under their eyes to mourn
over a year. They plowed this land
for us and for Lorine Niedecker
and they allowed us to dig
her grave in the swamp of the island
suddenly refilling with water
baptize and drink from the past.
Bank river word saga.
Chronicle living antiquity.

Irish Studies Conference, New York

The crowded Any Penny bar
at the base of Crane's long bridge.
It reminds me of Berryman
waving goodbye before leaping
into the frozen cold Minneapolis winter
solid for everyone inside
ignores grey clouds, sounds of freight trains
the northern edge of the world.

I remember a large University in my dreams
grand lecture halls, tables covered in white tablecloths
with coffee and tea, water, and scones.
Book tables and junk to stuff in free bags
people looking at programs and clocks, through windows.

I am on the fringe
searching for friendly faces
leaving chilled rooms into the heat of social hour.
My dreams look over railings
from small silent corners
parallel to bathrooms and escapes
nearly the green revolving door.

I will look for Liddy when I arrive.
His ghost still drinks in hotel bars.
I mention him to junior members of the club
work my way up to the bishops, cardinals,
popes – some now Pope emeritus
living on reading, writing volumes to fill
library carts and shelves, the stacks of war
and literature all forgotten, conveniently
not mentioned. Who has fallen to the ground
with me on my knees, fallen from grace
like the devil or other angels without proper direction.

Deals made in the lobby or on the street.
Someone is being consoled, a graduate student I believe.
I feel for her when I go outside to warm myself
think about fairies and the banshee's wish for stolen children.

Dream on, O perilous conference.
Awaken like the verse of springtime
and I will put my stanza inside your sequence.

March 2009

Airplanes Make Perfect Mobiles

And when the office was emptied into boxes
all that remained was a first aid kit in the closet.
This time you have come to teach and
the light creature kept silent in her soul
when we have parted therefrom and then
the war was over and all survived even with art.
Art is no comfort but an encyclopedia for the mind.
And at this time we all began to dance
with our hands.
                    And our hands became our
fathers' and our mothers' hands and our neighbors'.
And we forgot about ourselves. I wasn't surprised
when the songs came from the world and every
one did one courteous and we praised the gods
the authors and artists who break blue guitars
and are not responsible for the other interpretation
the other toys that meant birth busy hoping
our eyes gave no expression.
                    And those of us who
were clever enough or fool enough to forget
those times when we wished someone would
rush us to the hospital above the gargle of the
party the dreams of beds and stalwart love
in the heaven of afternoons. Love is more useful
than machines.
                    Look at our collage, this compulsion
in our bed and the quiet ones began to think
again and again and we all listened to the one
who made us, closely we heard the words
and looked both ways with Janus. A slow sound
station bound trains or maybe just breeze
independent of the breeze. Pick up those
guitar pieces in the room, the light in windows
the useful machine telling truth telling
life ambitious.

The Frank History

A most serious epidemic followed these prodigies.
While the Kings were quarrelling with each other again
and once more making preparations for civil war,
dysentery spread throughout the whole of Gaul.

      —GREGORY OF TOURS (AD c. 539 – 594),
        The History of the Franks

Isn't it always the way?

While we wait for kings and politicians
to make difficult and consequential decisions,
many are killed by simple and useless diseases
waiting for someone to act on issues of health care
and aid to the poor, inoculations, with simple faith
fervor, prayer for the scourge of illness.
We grow skeptical of life, when aristocrats
act the rescuer from our sins, our heresy
our latest fears of humanity until death us do part.

We turn toward history and toward religion, words
of the mystics, family bishops born on Saint Andrew's day
forgotten fables of mother's journey to Tours after his
consecration, cured by Saint Martin, fundraisers
with senatorial families, a long tradition of service
to the Catholic Church, that is to say of wealthy
Gallo-Roman landed gentry whose ancestors enjoyed rank
under the Empire and were extremely proud of the fact.

A whole while (a world and his wife later) what have we learned?
Thousands of years to sit and die alone in dark rooms
want of action, for the powerful to suffer.
To sweat out lingering explanations of the eternal mystery
feed on scraps left over separation of church and state;
two institutions linked by legal accomplishments
and concerning decisions rarely made in a timely manner.

Functioning Alcoholic

A glass in my hand makes an idea beautiful not fearful.

—JAMES LIDDY, *"Kubly's Farm, Drinks"*

Berryman, his eyes stare
filled to the rim
with wine stout Ireland.
He recited to publicans
if necessary.
Locals largely ignored
play on word
mostly slurs
heard it a million times before.
His beard moved letters
writing pint glasses
notes to girls worn
by the rain
…and…
Hart Crane danced all
the way to the sea
many times.
Underground rocks
silent island
letters lay ahead of him
his mother tried, his father tired.

Dylan Thomas
quipped and wore
backward suits
looked daily for
death, the proper hand.

Poe poet buried in a
grave deep down
sides and psalms of hell.

Baudelaire, be drunk!
Twin souls and
a modest allowance
mostly on virtue.

Let virtue pay all
the bills.
Mournful
solitude sings
a room only for saints.

Saints be drunk.

Hear them flying.

In the Apse was a Window of Red Glass which a Holy Man Had Placed There

Tristan called to his captors: "Lords, here is a chapel. For God's sake let me go in. My time is nearly at an end. I shall pray God to have mercy on me, for I have sinned greatly against Him. Lords, there is only this way in, and each of you is carrying a sword. You know that I cannot get out; I shall have to return to you. When I have ended my prayer I shall return to you as I say."

—Beroul, *The Romance of Tristan* (12 C.)

You know what happened (don't you?) Tristan walked inside
past the altar, the (red tinted) window behind, pulled toward him
with his right hand (might I add) to leap through the opening
escaping softly onto jagged rocks (for his lying sins) into the night
still afraid of being burnt or (worse) hanged before the assembly.
(I believe) he was thoughts (the entire time) of his love (for) his lover
Yseult, the church (of course) love for faith, faith of (devoted) men
souls left behind at the (wrong) opposite side of the small house
of forgiveness they came across. For we give him (immense)
credit because Tristan (fervently) studied his captors, prayed faith
made (them) believe he would kneel in (isolated) holy place, plague
coming days this uncertainty in lives of Christians scared into (signs and)
faith of times through (God) the only belief system they were aware
(in their own small world). (Daily) cries, tears of poor (hourly) trails
(sorrowful) flagellants. Tristan knew those fool foggy eyed (devoted)
souls – his captors. Flatter them with words (it is known) give them
confidence, the (joyous) love from God, large love grows need.
Loud love feels God upon his hand, his sentence that says us (we)
you and I are connected in mystery. I need to unburden my (awful)
sinful soul. His lies got bigger more boastful, teasing the (gullible)
guards with feeble (small) minds, sheepish brains molded in the word
the flock lonesome in the (barren) fields. He was (thoughts) all night
of his beloved, the tender (power) love that dare not touch the (forbidden)
fruit in the garden led by the hand, (everlasting) souls. Why had God
continued to show him (great) mercy? Why? He ran along the beach
with large strides, and he could hear the fire crackling (in the distance).
He had no mind to return (ever) and ran as fast as he could recalling
the wonder of his (devout) faith and desire to use it again and again
for his own (justified) end, the (sheer) comprehension of life works
with/without consequence. A mind's (limitless) knowledge (to learn)
how belief will mold fables, mysterious (and possibly) misleading fables.

On Finding a College Notebook
from Astronomy Class

Billions of years old, between twelve and eighteen billion years old
the universe and the earth only a quarter of life. Light is itself,
itself. Gamma rays and ultraviolet rays and visible inside invisible
penetrate atmospheres like humans penetrate each other. Both sides
famous scientists space as a measure of things: milli, mega, nano, giga.
Exponential notation with hypotheses and data time scale long radio
short radio wave center unfolding as bodies fill the stratosphere
astronomical units and coordinate systems with light year values.
Knowing the heavens, this celestial globe, mapping earth moves
Alpha and Beta, declination and right ascension for prime meridian
moves like Foucault's pendulum measure longest and shortest days
in diurnal motion of souls to swim up into the constellations.
Ancient Romans grew weary from sun spots and faces turned
toward and away from each other into sacrifices earth and moon,
lunar eclipse and the top wobbles, precession directly overhead
for time zones and ancient cultures full phases of the lunar surface
tell hours when we live our lives again and forever varied distance
of shadows form diamond ring effect, eruptions of gas and partial
explosions of love, for gravity is of apparent magnitude. Dim stars
and bright stars and helical rising from retrograde, each human
golden nose sniffing one another, body slide upwards for the laws
of inertia are dense and we are thick like terrestrial planets like
massive shift in tectonics forming our gracious and fleshy sphere
for organic beings are soil and rocky mountains in bodily energy
and gas and Calisto cratered surface almost ready to be unearthed,
no longer inert, a symptom of magnetic fields and large satellites
of chondrite nearly crashing into each other out of want and need
displacement laws and flares flow upwards and lost in a hot core.

Poem Written on James Joyce's Birthday (February 2, 2015)

What of muffinstuff
for these times?
Body language method
for loud noises-
lewd man whom history
has given climate. I ought
to state means by what
is proper, immodest forces
of the field
green light and clues
guide us to your home(s).
Sing (tenor) with me, Sunny Jim.
Top lines of poems
grand gesture places
someone packing-
up your trunk
clothes taken to a costumer
for better fitting.
Here comes every-
body like Adam and Eve
riverrun past Dublin environs
while slate out pride egos
filled high bodily
temperature
snake and fish
water and rock formation
for voyages with
love and lust, land
journey like oath word degrees
taken from
tongues and sounds
receding over the horizon.

Build a Poem

Girders among rubble
newspaper quotes, lines
ripped (stolen) from Eliot
a nod to Oppen, enclosed
folders with paperclips
rocks full of old holes.
Cut out paste them top
like mason building
brick wall one brick after
other concrete saint sea surge
of force under the joists.
Embed word in midst
to whittle down work
see chisel marks of con-
struction. Where are current
events? Here: young bartender
with black glasses, black t-shirt
dark tattoos. She keeps
me from concentrating
on the poem I build current
works verticle off the page.
Drink sip of beer. Back
to it, what is it? Social trauma
of increased modernization.
Relief map draft nail driven
thru pages into piece
of plywood geared in loose
mechanics of the world.
Staple revisions over
text. Meaning to be here
work plane as carpenter
and sailor. Beamstick
out, tear down history
recreate, pile up papers
find words stacked
real in life and what of
Crane's world with acetylene
sky burn into eyes and leak
across the laundry line stick
off page (metaphor) for

pipestem cleaners and
prose quotes linked to
verse pasted over early
lines. Out back in alley
filled with rubble text
longhand architect
doodle from building
upon building letter shifted
over large metal frame.
Elucidate shave off edge
but keep sharp corner
for ever time cut.
Hold thought in
shadow of Golden
Gate Bridge. No other
taste shall change that.

Wayfare

We went to meet
your beautiful friends
with smooth skin
at cafes/sidewalks
and lovers strolled
in light worlds
similar to westerns
now enchanting
intimate with deciduous
trees to wake forests.
We painted their
shimmering light
the play often thru
lilting and falling
(wet) leaves.
In autumn we moved
on rivers pulling
boats called skiffs
where short bows
held stern. We did
not know them
to find stability
among the rubble
and the ruins.
We passed under
bridges to know
hotels with bars
and stayed to drink
recovering
ourselves different
from our lives
at home.
We shared
in heavy
outdoor field work
of farm life
and, as Mary Oppen
wrote, "we were
shocked that the old
life had qualities
that some newer
ways had lost."

Thoughts in an Empty Bar on Tuesday Afternoon, the First Day of Autumn

Don't believe the darlings
instead believe the treasured jewels
off the coast of Havana while
multitudes move like wild fire
burning in the sand. Poetry wars
are for people who trust words.
Trust the flowers for the sun.
Ideologues are forever feigning
interest in our bodies thrust to
and fro. Flotsam and jetsam
throw faith for narrow senses.

The Nurse of Enchantment
(On Reading Helen Adam)

About to take a walk I stopped and saw her dance
lunge to us a wand made of ballads and ghost worlds.
She held us in her palm for hours, a lethal woman
for all to fear. Her sexuality, her sadism, her jealous affairs
tightly wound in fear; *he was a gentleman*, she said. *I regretted
his death.* She wore a spangled garter, a candle flame in hand.
We danced to the bar to buy cigarettes from the machine.
In the lobby of the old hotel she whispered later into my ear
a dead heart that raced downstairs and made abandoned towns
seem full of people and martyrs. The female saints came screaming
out of her and her white shoes were pastoral subjects. She was
to tell the truth, not very friendly, walk along indolently
leaning on each other's shoulders. What sorcerers shall fill
up her blank book for wild young sages a special kind of madness.

Riverwest, This Part of the World

I'm sitting in the Polish Falcon, afternoon rain.
And, yes I am drinking a beer and talking
to the bartender, listening to his multitude of stories.
He tells them slowly, with intense feeling
mostly about Washington D.C., a recent trip, how
easy to navigate busses and the subway system.
His name is Dennis and I imagine him like
an advertisement, a man with a smile
and a thumbs up on a billboard for a destination
I remember visiting as a child. Perhaps he
also works for the tourism board.
He asks if I want a second beer. I nod
as he begins to pour another one and I listen
to the kids playing outside and think about this bar
this area. I am looking to get something to eat
up the road perhaps at Nessun Dorma or maybe
Fuel Café and I think about when I lived here
and spent time at Mad Planet dancing with reckless
graduate students (as I was a reckless graduate
student at the time) and spending afternoons reading
in bars, writing poems at small wooden tables
outside cafés or benches on sidewalks. There are
wide streets here with parked cars all leading to small
duplexes or walkups with little balconies
and small shops next to empty Catholic churches
and Eric lives a few blocks over probably doing
more renovations on his tri-plex, the place never done.
Much help and amounts of free work from his father.
And then Paul comes into the Falcon and soon Eric too.
We talk about the death of Bill Meyer what
Jim told us about his fateful stress test. David
relayed the funeral arrangements, a few weeks away.
It saddens us for a moment and there is a silence
for Bill followed by an endless sea of stories
mostly from Liddy's Epiphany party every year
a new feel, a desired time with friends.
Then Dennis hears what we are saying
to each other and gives us a free shot to toast Bill.
We raise our glasses, drink them down together
and the whiskey is smooth in our throats

as the rain starts hitting the front windows.
I look into my glass in remembrance
in reverence, in requiem for past lives,
past and future places like Riverwest
where the birds will always sing (even in winter)
and we can together drink away our fears.

II

Letters to James
(with love and admiration)

Speak, God of visions, plead for me
and tell me why violence answers love.
There are only two reasons for travelling: restaurants
and neglected public monuments. There are two reasons for
keeping alive: being in love
and ambiguity.

—JAMES LIDDY
"Requiem for a Non-Croppy"

I.

Dearest James — How is it you are still in my mind
when you moved like supreme grace much in the days
and nights of our fair city. Milwaukee is not Dublin
in the 1960s, but your sweating forehead and salmon
coloured sweater now matches the pink swelter of east
side parties and bars, bier gartens as a consolation
for the soul. Continue to say prayers for me. I have lost
my way to the Benedictines via the Jesuits. Social justice
is on the lips of all Jesuits boys, taking selfies with Pope
Francis. That Jesuit boy is aware of his humble past
while people from the world over look through hallways
of old cracked stone staircases. He twists himself into
puzzles and brain games while doing a pirouette
for the girls' school down the road. They laugh riotously.
Someday I will be able to repay you and praise you.
Life will be rejoicing and bows/handshakes after we sit
and eat dinner of salted fish on a balcony overlooking Ronda
gorge. I just heard an interview on the radio with Seamus
Heaney. He is now dead so as to not bore anyone.
But he did say something about prayer and poetry
which made me think of you (and also the Pope).
Your devotion is to the mass of poems / drinks with
Hartnett and friends (poets) among lives. Supreme
goodness, his holy service, continual praise and thanksgiving.

II.

Brother James —
How did you know I would like to hear about Simone Weil. I have
become obsessed with her I fear and no longer can I stop writing
letters. I imagine a factory in heaven with all the workers stopping
to chat her up, bring her some food or soup, possibly a prayer book.
I keep thinking about her near conversion at the high Mass and her
notes about the cloud of unknowing. What was behind those small
glasses of hers? She seems concentrated, writing about the *Iliad*
and its force. The lord who is to judge us. There is another arts
faculty making life size papier-mâché models of her and placing
them in stairwells and behind doors in the basement of the cafeteria.
I must stop for a drink at the Rathskeller and see who is behind
the bar. Could it be an angel? Perhaps it is Simone praying for our
souls in written language, all religions, looking for souls on
windowsills of our world, head aches from our silent nights.
She spoke sweetly and gave us the habit.

III.

My James —Who is to be around when I die? Children, animals
drunk ex-girlfriends waiting to dance on the dirt covering my grave?
Maybe I will be cremated as to not arouse lines of communicants
lining up for a chance to take a swipe at this feeble body. I have
been thinking a lot about death lately and hope that it is simply
a phase. But it concentrates the mind and only the right amount
of drinks can do that otherwise. I was a good billiards player after
three beers; more and the game was over before I fell on the floor
to down more. I have been reading books and writing about Orpheus
shiftless. More pint glasses before I write ideas down. Late
night dark desk writing about a friar, tied up and put on show
in the street at the gates of the monastery. He had an affair, didn't
gain more merit in the eyes of his divine majesty. Insults and foul
slurs laid waste to him. Will he survive?
I secretly pray for many people when I can. Don't tell my relatives
they might think I have lost my edge. But I must say that I cannot
think of other ways to be devotional. I am afraid to pray on death
and I rarely write about it. Poems are prayers for angels who
give alms to the muses. I fall in love with them every day, leave
out a book to sleep into, the letters form shapes and sudden
like the butterfly I fall to my knees, progress in spiritual ways:
self-love, self-will, self-interest. Who will grave my ghosts?

IV.

Dear James — You have seen the light
of my mind. Charles Baudelaire was drunk
often and he gave us poems to make us remember
our prayers. Steam night Paris must
have been something to see even with disease
and poverty run amok. I gave some money
to the poor box at the Church of the Gesu and wrote
instructions on how it was to be given
to Baudelaire. I wonder if the priests will look
for him on Wisconsin Avenue among the people
waiting for the bus and the men pushing
shopping carts toward the I-43 freeway entrance.
It might be Jesus who is waiting in black clothes
of a poor man, a hoody pulled over his eyes
dirt under the fingernails of promise, poet men
wrinkling their way into the downtown library.
The smells of stale cigarettes and soiled shirts.
Library book and coffee shop had a copy of your
Selected Poems for sale. I bought and left it
on the steps, wrote a note, told of its inner light.
Donations like money for reading and for the masses.
I wonder what Alan Hayes is doing right now. I hope
he is relaxing among the reeds of Galway. I must
say that sometimes life brings us happiness
and excellence followed by pressing duties.
Baudelaire felt that and spilled precious words
on the floor of brothels. He was the son and heir
to forgotten and eternal. I pray for his knowledge.

V.

Mentor James – Old courage teacher. I walked through the east side
yesterday looking for a coffee shop that I now believe must be gone.
How lives change when you're away. Dublin seems more sinister somehow.
Suddenly I found myself at Co. Clare ordering a beer. Stodgy Milwaukee.
How that place shines in the day with bankers and business men. One
hotel where we could go to get away from all the preachers of life.
It still startles me when I see 21 year olds ordering pints. For some reason
I always thought Ireland was full of old men. But now it is as tolerant of
youth as is Milwaukee. How it has changed in the autumn of our tears.
No longer does it smell like Fest city, but some kind of sausage factory.
What did George Oppen say about California? *Streaming with the waves
of the Pacific going past.* Lake Michigan has fewer waves, but they
pass the shores of UWM with students surfing them, conquered on the
beaches of their minds. Bright simpleness and strangeness of the
sands and cold bodies waiting for warmth. Busy harbors make ponderous
odors and that small dark architecture on the south side of the city.
How old we all are and how the spring water gushes forth in the spring.
I heard a rumor about the owner of At Random. He hides around/behind
dumpsters at night and watches his patrons go to their cars, phones
in hand, slightly drunk. He waits to see if they can navigate the steering
wheel and radio at the same time. A people watching peeping Tom.
Doesn't everyone drive drunk in Milwaukee? Especially band
members crowding out of the Cactus Club. Bus drivers of the world
unite and take over.

VI.

Dearest James — Hart Crane has become quite interesting. I think
of his suicide, contemplate the pressures of family. I am not sure of his thoughts
for his eyes seem dark in the daytime in pictures taken by friends. I suppose
his mother was concerned about her boy, son of a candy maker, useless life savers
a father, the smell of money in his veins. His mother busied herself playing against
the candy boss, sweet meat maker of Ohio with buckets of maple syrup and sugar
jars filled with joy. I found enlightening thoughts in Crane's letters and poems,
words disclose to us directions out of greater service. There is silence in them
a calm of the mind, cares to find flight. His letters are golden words, wonderful fear
about getting a job — heaven knows he's miserable now. He likes himself and
desires to live in the shadow of his bridge forever. Those high girders must
have seemed dizzying, a terrible fear to put down on paper and relive
every day of his life. Those who are weaker are more preoccupied. He
always commanded his wishes and sorted them into flocks of birds waiting
to exit the sky, trembling in the sun with no prophets to rely on. What went
through his mind on those trips by boat to the south seas and his mother's
plantation to write and imagine. Was he mortified by God's opinions?
I would hope to talk to locals after hurricanes/floods, wishing to be servants
of the world and the word. I suppose he wanted some attention. And attention
from you poet James is better than the love of Christ, also more inviting.

VII.

My dearest James — A week of very mad rushing, obedience to spiritual
texts. Hardly time to reminisce about whirl and drinks with Carolyn Forché
on top floors of the Pfister Hotel drinking German beer and wine
among Wisconsin Cheddar flight, apple chutney, drunken strawberries.
How I could feel the night to notice the blood moon over Milwaukee.
She dazzled me with her stories of AWP and book construction and advice
from foolish old men. How young she seems to me. But poets always
somehow remain young. She told me she could keep teaching for another
ten years. How I would miss her classroom as I do yours. Everywhere
I see classrooms in fields and bars, in flights of a heron's wing and soft
twilight sun too bright for the day. It is a sacrifice to the salvation of souls.
Writers are sensual past. Inside the docks of graves in Ireland. We spoke
of that too and I mentioned the usual writers: Joyce, Beckett, Yeats.
She told me of Galway in her youth and the west of Ireland her favorite
parts. It all seemed so Greek in admiration. I had no doubts of the pleasure,
the prayers. I am obedient with nothing to sacrifice. And Oppen came to her
reading when she was only 26 years old. How I would give to see that
as I see the Russian waves of vodka in my eyes and hearing stories
of how we should learn to love one another. How I want to give over
and revive myself. There is a necessary bond between the young and the old,
the ones in between. She told me to have that all. I was reminded of you,
your connections between generations. Mentors are certain Gods.

VIII.

Dearest James – I went up north to sing in the woods among the students
and bridges over gorges, pot smoke rising from the forest floor. I love the tables
up in Siberia, they also sing at night and cry tears in the morning like poets
and Orpheus upon discovering the sudden death of Eurydice. Snake bite sonorous
with lute in hand and bodies shaken from his fingers, his voice under spells.
Spicer said he made the king of hell weep, the proudest boast and the shell
of living creatures dancing on the edge of the world. And I have flown and made
marches in the night spilling milk on the starry floor where three headed dogs lap
up as we look into mirrors. Sunlight and lamplight in sadness like a handkerchief.
My heart is the air and recites a song for me, winds in the sky like beautiful
poems and notes (letters) until the Ciconian Maenads tear him apart, tattoos shine
like sons. Ask Lorca who is the real in poems, rough ground. I would prefer to drink
Hoegaarten in Romans on the south side and fight for freedoms, sounds of distorted
guitar. Words are everlasting great, strange goodness in the fields of the mind
and the drugs and booze filtering in the system die early, crazy and leave a good
looking oeuvre; poetry for the living and the dead. Crane, Spicer, Berryman, O'Hara
like Orpheus weeping in the afterlife over again when nature creates itself perfect.

IX.

Mentor James – This letter has many ghosts in it. Ghosts never leave behind traces
even though we feel them every day. Kind of like pinball when we lose our places
knocked around pushing us to land in the gutter of lost chances, they fall into oblivion.
I seem to remember a small scene long ago when we drove to a small town in Michigan
for a conference and got lost. You asked if we could go find Madonna's High School
and look at the football field. I peered down at the map and almost ran into another car.
The other driver yelled at us, called us Wisconsinites in a derogatory tone. The sun blazed
from behind blue clouds after we drove down another street and came to train tracks –
grown over, almost abandoned. We stopped at the Lincoln bar nearby and saw a wide
range of people. Contrary to popular belief the state isn't all white. Thank God, we sighed
together. Then a train went barreling past and you ran outside, told me how we were going
to jump it, take a trip all the way to California. Favorite boxcars movement into memory
as children and Kerouac. You were jubilant. This must be the train headed west Romantic
life hitched to pools in grey sky, road men, transients trading sardines for stories and fun
with the steady hatted places, a question of purpose – classes in art history pretending
to think it over for a while. You looked from above like an angel in the sky and I thought
you were writing a poem, a poem with the mention of a writer or two, a drink from
the bar, a train vanishing into blonde US landscapes. But soon we headed back
to the car and drove into civilization, found another bar and had another drink, now
with more crowds and noise. "Some adventure" you said. I agreed and thought and took
another sip of my beer while I watched you speak and I taught myself with wide eyes
and windmill constant steadiness of a student – reverence and devotion, feeling days
passing by like bending grass in the field outside of town. Tremble with us. Coal mine
roads stop for thirty minutes from four hour drive as we fell backwards into history.

X.

Our James – Have you forgotten about me?
I hope this letter finds you well in heaven with
all of your angels. I think about you more in the days
after teaching. I walk home or take a bicycle covered
in dirt from the Root River Parkway. 20,000 years
in the making where arrowheads find themselves
buried under rocks from the previous ice age. Old things
remind me of poetry as do new things – it electrifies
the conversation between generations. I mentioned
to relatives a while ago, how I considered you a good friend
all those years and they laughed. Asked how I could
be friends with someone who was so much older.
I said it was because you were actually quite young –
young at heart, young in spirit, youth in poetic form.
The days we spent in Dublin and Madrid too always
informed me. The surroundings of course held mystic
view and large lesson. But it was you who directed
us to the spots of the seasons, the place of largest lessons.
Thank you for those days, the laughs we had on river
trips down the Mississippi, the raft my little red car.
Two angels on a river boat cruise with red faced cherubs
arguing with devils. Throwing arrows into our hearts.
Worship from afar is always songs and how I woke you
with Morrissey singing from the driver's seat to hear
angel voices flowing from car windows. I learned more
from you on a trip to southern Illinois and in bars.
The classroom ringing out under stars. Learn to climb the
gossip tree and hold on for dear life, express real feelings.
They can rival the kisses on your lips, the teacher
still spilling from your cup. Drink it in and breathe.

XI.

Mentor James – Now John Berryman, a poet to model in our dreams.
I have been reading about his time in Ireland. Henry on the Emerald Isle
drinking with the locals and trying to avoid getting caught eyeing the women
about town. He once said that the narrator of *The Dream Songs* was not
the poet, not him. But Henry admits to being in Ireland writing the last of them.
Henry dreaming and praying to the Irish Gods and an awkward kiss of beer
breath left on shades of grass he walked over on his way home to stone rock
cottage. Videos of him reading while drunk surfaced a few years ago, asleep
with his secrets. Henry in Ireland to John underground. Rest well with a bottle
of whiskey next to you in the coffin. High-jinks made higher by booze, rough
journey and sweet silence. He has crowned my travels and wasted my days
ever so slightly for men of all ages will be my compass. Shade to shade
the shadows of great poets trip along my tongue to one side of my mind.
Thank you James, thank you Henry pussycat, thank you shadow of Yeats.

XII.

James – A serious one. I am depressed today
hearing news stories of children shot accidentally
while playing. Fearful like the job market. I ponder in Latin
hourly with you as a muse-guide to my mental health.
Epistulae ad Familiares.
Life is sturdy and beautiful, full of wasp nests
offers to avoid when we most want to hold them
in our hands. I turn my head to the window,
the walled spring faking its way to happiness
trivial triumphs, defeats. I swim back to the father
of duty, the work of 1000 autumns, the tide pushes back
against me all the time even when I win, I don't win.
Still I am resolute often, steadfast in my resolve.
But who cares except me, maybe my sons, maybe my heirs
like horses they graze in the fields of the earth
long lost grasses eaten up with little patches fought over
for seed. Plant us in the ground again, water us, make us grow
we need to salvage the words from the spirit, the tides
of waters flow. Beckett began his journey of the mind
and now we finish with our verbal hell. Pray for us James.
Pray that we lose ourselves in the dark night of mystery.

XIII.

Dearest James — How I think of Liam this morning
and his calligraphy. I also think of your sister, Nora
in her nursing home outside Wexford. All roads lead to
Wexford and all roads lead to the bedroom where people
live and die and are surrounded by nurses and questions.
The eternal is full of majestic powers and having a beer
in a pub with Liam sounds like heaven and sings like
heaven. It must be heaven. The utter husk of the spirit
feels, expresses ideas, identity. The world breaks open
at my feet and friends and greatness abound. I feel lucky
to have known you and your friends. There is a purple
sound from trumpets when I visit your museum. They
announce the regal presence of poet gods, muse shining
windows covered in words and raided by the spirit. We
all live here, call it life like strangers on the street, the dark
faces we cover in the noon light. I say we shall be drunk
at lunchtime forever and embrace our cool street barbarians.
Drive on sleepless, the whispering watch of bodies swaying.

XIV.

Dear James – I am thinking of Lorine Niedecker this morning
when the light shines on the faces of young poetry students. She
is magical, an inspiration to Wisconsinites. How I would have
liked to drink with her or just be around her. Her words are
certain life and bluest water, always water in surrounding regions
of the mind. I think that her star is rising like Jupiter's moon Io,
a large goddess hovering in the sky with orbits in the far reaches
of space, connecting body and soul. Somehow she also seems
forgotten at times, a little voice in a big place left on the edge.
Like the plants in her part of the world, let her ideas perennially
grow, let the noise of linnets wings inspire Yeats, the symbol
of dark and light, the image of dinner parties and cabbage soup
for all to smell. Delicious flower of Black Hawk Island
young daughter with whom to sow the seeds of word light.
She was and is next year's labors. Abandon the idea rich
and pack alabaster vases and bridle bits, her parts of land
sinking slowly into the Rock River. Nurse her pump lids over
small holes in her walls and begin again, the seeds of
the senega root. They grip tightly to the earth, never letting go.

XV.

To James – Lilting Liddy: teacher, builder, crafter we love so much clay
in the hands of your warm heart. The poem begins to glimmer, to form in the mind.
I remember your office hours in the bar in the last few hours before last call
and advice and what to read to call home the sound of everlasting good words
reverberating in our ears close to perfection. Words are everlasting greatness
strange in the field of the mind. Song like poems do well with drugs and booze
and we will die early and young. Corpses never write another scrap. But I would
like to be found under rocks in the new century, discovered like the night after
underground taverns close and we had been in there all day. Students in moments
not life time learners. They fight it after college. Most talk of how to make more
money and watch television of elections or fights or politics and sport Saturdays
in the autumn. Spicer wanted to taste the lemon in the poem, the sour bitter
smells of citrus, the real life in taste and being. He would run breathless from his
apartment to search for someone to show the poem to. Now that's devotion to a craft.
What is the "real" in poetry but small jackhammers pounding in our mind. Trucks
drag images into poems over rough ground with long ropes taught to stretch
over drums and crates. I would prefer to drink Guinness in a bar and savor life
and some of this we will never have and others will have less. Poetry is freedom
and the mind deserves it. I had friends to which I dedicated poems. You are
someone whom I dedicate my life, poems with words and love to love oceans.

III

Ephemeral

Heaven made this place, also, assisted by men,
great men & weird. I see their shades move past
in full daylight.
The holy saints make the trees' tops shiver,
in the all-enclosing wind. And will love last
further than tonight?

—JOHN BERRYMAN
"Dream Song 313"

Ireland and Beyond

LETTER TO BERNIE IN CO. WEXFORD
WRITTEN 4:15 A.M. IRISH TIME

What tree grows in my throat
for summer parades on distant nights
and slumber wakes to catch the rising dawn.
We love the human beings who love
to serve us drinks. She is populating the small
town with looks and brilliant lights
for towns people strong enough to return
to Top Shop for curry chips.
I proclaim this history
made by small eyes of O'Rafferty's
the small yellow window
tearfully remember for the waiting
fire, the small tree I see
it disappear.

HOLY TRINITY OF IRISH WRITERS

Father Yeats
Son and Brother Joyce
Holy Ghost Beckett

POEM FOR JAMES JOYCE

What is the age of the soul of man?
—James Joyce, *Ulysses*, Episode 14: Oxen of the Sun

Ashplant cane
heaventree
knight of the razor.
Smell linden trees
along the street
cry for the girl
down the lane.

I am going blind
slowly. By streets
and oil lamps
glowing in the corner
on the stairs.
Every step my soul
seems to sigh.
Amend my life
through regions
of sticky gloom.

WHAT I HAVE LEARNED FROM STANISLAUS JOYCE

I see discussions filled with brief and sharp comment
(possibly) stolen from a former source
and youth was often the means, the eternal
thought in the mind of God.
No watertight compartments of the soul
no enemy of free thinking.
Simply the joy of the living.
His mother had spoken comfortingly
of her love for him when he was a child.
Closer is she than breathing; nearer than hands and feet.
As I had something to say to its reshaping
I can affirm this without hesitation.
The little flower of genius is the labor
of the ages and the re-birth of the world's interpreter.
Fear can also be vivid in early impressions.
Epiphanize how it left indelible traces on his soul.

DUBLINERS

Joyce still story
teach us
morals and
mirrors
lived with
tangled hair
under gas
ring tale lights

BENEFICIUM

I ask myself this question: what would have happened to me if I had not met
you in the morning of my life? I would have stayed lawyer and hung myself
writing prose. But words alone are certain god.

—James Liddy, *"A Memoir of Parnassus"*

O poet/mentor with strong audacity
angelic impact
manifest
Irish poetry and otherwise.
Aid, embed, encourage
the young poets.
For youth has many dreamers
many familiars...
Meetings and lunches, readings or events
a push onto a stage
nearest the actors and writers
song of patron muse.
Thank you for grace
and direction. No other life
could give such dreams of Parnassus.

James Liddy Comments Excerpted from an Interview with John Montague in TCCR

Doyle! Peter Doyle!
What about Edward Carpenter?
The grey hair makes him look like a Jesuit.
(Holding up rosary beads) Will you bless this for us, John?
They never wrote a bad review of each other!
Maybe it was because you are both male and female at the same time too, John!
That's right. I was there. You were a ghost, and Yeats was a ghost, and John Berryman became a ghost shortly afterwards.

Poem for Liam O'Connor

"The Lion Sleeps Tonight" sung on the crowded train from Dublin.
Another drink before casual dinner? Of course. Another drink with you.
Always.

A Night with Liam

We met on the corner near Grogan's Castle
Lounge after dinner with friends and tramping
around Temple Bar with students where pint
glasses were placed at the corner dark curbs
for barmen to pick up in the glow of morning.
It was grand to see your face again and I never
saw Joan happier reminiscing about Liddy's
kitchen and nightcaps in dark light. We talked
in between sips and sang songs, entered the land
of the kings, delights of the world and charity.
He that is righteous, let him be righteous still.
Let soul be cast into the body and believe in
nothing else. A unit does not change its nature.
I only feel esteem, see the words in the air,
a table and pints between our unity and infinity.

POEM FOR NORA IN WEXFORD

Smells like Coolgreaney when the plaice arrives.
Jim did much of the cooking. Some port and talk
outside in the garden before and after dinner.
German stove with odd settings, heat cook broil.
Later, lads at Mary's singing song, a bawdy one.
Someone recited a poem and we frowned, Eric's
mind acute. We chose our own words down from
blue smoke off the Wexford hills. Time stops
as it well should when we pray this blessed state.

EXCERPT FROM A BIOGRAPHICAL NOTE

After leaving Oxford Noyes went to London
and very soon began writing poetry
that became popular.

THE SEINE OVERFLOWS

Is Paris Burning?
No, today it's drowning.

POEM FOR AIRPORTS

Wait lines
and more lines wait
fawns look up
from the brook.
Queue in this new world
these cold window suns
and sound high pitched
rev ears in brightness.
When we cross
the Rubicon without shoes
or belts and our hands
above our heads
reach for oasis—
recombobulation area.
Fix and shine
stop adjust
and swollen eyes.
For now, I am
no less confused.

BEERS OF THE WORLD

Tour yourself!
Feel every mountain and crevasse.
Drunk exploration with
in perfect bars preferably
asking not for the usual
but surprise me.
Determine new detours
life and patronage
friends turn to lovers.
Explore yourself and declare
yourself, people composing songs
with lyres like Orpheus
strumming that lust.
Each other moving rocks
trees, the king of hell himself.

Midwesterners

New Glarus Settler

Hilarius Wild was the original
19th century party animal.
He was often seen around town
verbally promoting
Swiss/German beer and tourism.

Pilgrimage

He took the long walk to Woodstock,
Illinois and looked for Jesuits.

Hebron, Illinois

Father Marquette stands under the elm
at the village limits and looks on with amazement.

Wednesday October 15, 2003

Shall I compare thy beauty to a scenic view?
Thou art rarer than an 82 degree October day in Northern Wisconsin.

Rule #27 for Teaching at an Evangelical Christian School with a Seminary

God convenes his meeting every Thursday morning.
Faculty and student meetings are strongly discouraged during Chapel.
The Atheist/Agnostic Club must reschedule.

MYSTICAL DAYDREAMING AT THE AUTUMN FACULTY MEETING

Sounds up to heaven echo in cavernous ocular spaces.
The closets are filled with crucifixes.
In the libraries are the mystics, praying.
Flagellation followed by solitude and silence.
People whose souls grew weary of the time,
self-denial for the glory of God. No light dark rooms
and sins for a century of asceticism, tears of blood.
She can still make me cry determination. You are forgiven
again, forever. Forgiven inside a meditative heart
where souls mine the children who become adults
where the blind stirring of love becomes a sharp dart.
In time you will learn to hammer the cloud
and the darkness above you. It is by love
we can be caught and held.

The Gnaw of Hunger

Night I went down to the pantry in the kitchen. Don't like all the smells
in it waiting to rush out.
What was it she wanted? The Malaga raisins. Thinking of Spain.

– James Joyce *Ulysses* Episode 8: Lestrygonians

CAUL FAT

Line my bread pan
with your love and
tie up the edges
of trim, snipped clean.

Slow roasted
cooked evenly
in a hot oven
not to simply melt the fat
but to meld
with a swallow-able
crouton topping.

Lusty grease
makes love gravy
spread with the world's
love flesh.

SOFT CHEESES

Pray for cows to give good milk
grass fed from the diet of rolling hills
North of France climate.
Monks make meaty brie for Lent.
Everyone deserves a little reward.

FORTUNE COOKIE

You will be pleasantly surprised
soon.

ÊTRE À LA HAUTER

Suffice it to say
mustard could be the only
condiment I need

ONION HEADLINE

Man Accidentally Eats Packet Marked "Do Not Eat"

Nocturnal Prayer/Ambitious Meditation

The poet's body lay, yet by a miracle the River Hebrus / Caught head and lyre as they dropped and carried them / Midcurrent down the stream. The lyre twanged sad strains, the dead tongue sang; funereally the river banks and reeds / Echoed their music.

Ovid, *Metamorphoses. XI. 62-65.*

POETRY AND MUSIC

Poetry and Music have much in common.
However, I do prefer a *Selected Poems* to a *Greatest Hits* collection.

RELIGION AND POLITICS

Which great decision you will make?

TEENAGE LOVE LETTER FOUND IN A USED BOOK

Have a lovely evening/morning of paper writing.
I'll miss you when I'm all alone tonight.
I wouldn't worry about losing anyone over break
or after break or even before break.
Tomorrow, find me as soon as you can.

IMPULSE COLUMN

All of the facts, none of the guilt.

TV LAND IRONY

Producers give extreme home makeovers to the downtrodden
those denied home loans.
Many viewers watch the excitement unfold from a slumlord's rental property.

Home Shopping Network beams round the clock,
competes for ratings against TV doctor shows.
Today's topic: chronic shopping addiction.

Video Game Haiku

Far worse than TV
channeling infinity.
Hands on waste of time.

Seesaw

Two
for the money
nay love
drinks and the dinner
suffused with
sex and
tax deductions
with friends
or without
altar courtly love.
Seesaw
o seesaw
tell me
the truth
of daily flowers
a crush
and a smoke
back to
loving ourselves
day in
and day out
of our minds.

IV

Je suis comme ça

> —SAMUEL BECKETT, *Waiting for Godot*

Less than anyone are we secure in order,
because we create order it cannot contain us–

> —GEORGE OPPEN, Daybook III

What composite asymmetrical image in the mirror then
attracted his attention?

The image of a solitary (ipsorelative) mutable (aliorelative) man.

> —JAMES JOYCE
> *Ulysses* Episode 17: Ithaca

The History of Finger Painting

Art house dance club rock
world patient ears.
Everything speaks to us, everything sings to us.
Blame it on youth.

Remember time, sketch
sidewalks and street lights, dialogue of dramatic
overtones. TV and telephone pole art
leaning table art, symbiotic dance number art
boy leotards strutting to the plucks of Paganini art.

Trips to museum see paint
calms our mind
for once instead of fast pace animals
virtuous groan businessmen.

Picasso pushed art into new faces.
Wilde crafted words into impressionable
drama and poetry for the sake
of art freedom embraced. Hang paint cans from boat sides
whitewash fences mural color
saxophones visualize sound
drawn round scribbles on dark paper stick people
with large heads, round feet.

Art always looks for the trouble with us
distortion expression pushed reason. There is no reason
what reason do you need?
Mysterious tapers burn silently above our heads
leak ideas bend moments into sight
and we cry in the corner
of the room
kids bow heads, reverent, waiting for
next muse formulate history of knowledge — we don't know
the faults of ourselves.

Art for escape four walls like
kind elephants plotting our jailbreak
with few casualties
questions in halls
of our horrible burden
our glorious flaws.

Beast and Mankind Dream of Costa Rica

Tico time blends animal kind and rainforest forever relaxed
drinks and feasting with jaguars late December equatorial morning.
Books and games with sun white faced monkeys on balconies all day
smelling grill grease, our meal at last slow dusk of fish and shrimp
hungry hands and light fixed a fall over large pacific rocks, wind—
sailors can view rich coast life, the gentle species of Central America.
Now, banana blight eradicated, coffee beans with ocean breeze
blown far off palm oil dangers shadowed by snakes, sinful
poisonous tall stick machetes and crocodiles under bridges.
Bicycles hide the shade from backs, long legs of jungle.
Dirt roads carved with workers used as mules for tourists
to zip line mountainsides strung by insect explorers. Chest
thumping optional. Immense leaves with small pools of dew.
We animals watch heavenward, water trees in the clouds.
Most days we are aroused by ghosts of saints, weather
wet from the heavens, sky dark — light instinct, small faith found
on basilica floor prayers to La Negrita. We, reverent, solemn
each of our bended knees round and whole, like the sphere.
Cartago's world runs miles past the farmers, industry
for Quepos fans us with the flame, the holy heart and
sweaty rebirth in heat Manuel Antonio Christmastime.
We hear howlers in the distance, under new moons.
We claim and believe as Toucans sit and listen quietly—
geckos geometric on the windows, lizards jump from stone patio
to thick brush. Soon, for the Feast of the Epiphany,
we will north Midwest home again without immense yellow sun,
blink my eyes with God and beasts in fever weeks to Milwaukee.
Negative nine grey degrees as I drive to the store—
milk has gone sour. Football fans stock up for the big game.
They rumble from the snow. I float with my cart. I am a dream
of a sloth asleep on shade branch tree, refusing to come down.

Outside Trip to the Dalí Museum, Figueres Spain

Are we where
Joan, are we where?
Train ride full
wedding bride rain
on brick street
sudden theater melted
with cactus.

Garden of hotels in Barcelona
on the other side
into affluent tropical wine
long alley of islands.
We take the submarine.

Run into me
his mustache and
grave part of
festival seating.

The walls streaked
red over harbors and guitars
sing lonely eyed
patrons buy flowers
clap hands with
cork fingers.

Crew cowers its way
to long basement
cling to walls
of cafes cold light
for small dogs
on the plaza.

He walks a marsupial
on a leash
looks into the sun
covered with white sheets.

His face above
in squares backing up
like a ship's mast
blinding us as glitter
from the sea.

This bright day
dreams heat lines
disperse for beers.

Adrift on a beach
in clear night
under small palm trees.

I remember cracked heavy
morning
and our safe crystal pool.

Artmovie JC and the Origin of the Strawberry Moon

Outside, a rock table talking of books and postcards
before skips to the Haggerty Museum through glass doors
to wander, ponder, and talk. Slowly Bliss, Idaho black and
white pictures next to jars with jelly beans, Bunny Peeps.
I think of childhood, feel innocent with JC, young again
like always learning something new.

There are flickers of light and smiles – movies flow images
of the Snake River above the main gallery with a short
melodrama, a Douglas Sirk inspired film and dialogue lifted
from Samuel Beckett plays. We wait on the bench and love
how we feel alone together. Two spinning tops in the world
slowly nudging us closer.

We look at the green digital moon in the corner and JC
mentions the strawberry moon tonight. We make plans to stare
together later with beers outside. Then we push through curtains
like a secret hedgerow leading into the next room.

JC watches the Frankie Latina movie looking smart in her
moon matching green dress. And I am looking at her, at the art
the curve of a neck, the line of a brow, the smile of her eyes.
Our minds turn toward art, opened by art as I stand next to her.

And now we are both together a work of art inserted into a painting.
Colors move slow like the light ray from above. And now we are
in the movie broadcast on a large white wall. We stand on a street
under industrial Milwaukee as a beige 1970s Pacer makes turns into
underpasses sit crushed vans shot from many angles. Other museum
patrons watch us age ever slowly, repeat our scene.

But we stay still – young and new, excited to learn of these moments.
Timeless like art, slow sounds when two minds collide and the rest
of the world comes to watch us evolve together as a complex image
arriving like an epiphany. A new moon tinted red because in youth
the artful moon doesn't have to obey the rules.

Poem after Spicer

There are boys on the pavement sunning themselves, thoughts
run away from night before days, bars with darkness.

Baudelaire drinks/thinks to himself and ponders voyage bodylove
under golden lights streaking through the sky.

Light crawls up the side of bluff walls terribly hot
summer pours through with brandy trickling down the rocks.

Is there anything hidden here? Frenzied animals escape
lower trenches in oceans, wet from lust.

No coast and trees to anchor wisdom.
We discover ourselves.

In Bed with Joan and Jack Gilbert

So he will hammer me deep into that rendering. Knowing blindly
there is something to get.

—JACK GILBERT, *"Threshing the Fire"*

And Joan is silent beside me
asleep like the Jack Gilbert book
on my night table
speaking of "the days and nights…
the brevity of life."

And a woman I met at the reading
in Milwaukee
with Fran and Andrea
who said she had lived
with Jack briefly
for roughly a year in the 1970s.

And I asked if she had any stories
she said, "Oh, too many!"

Letter to Cynthia Belmont

Dearest Cyn—
I am sorry that I am not near you right now
when I have just bought the *Collected Poems*
of Jack Gilbert. I remember your stories of escorting
Jack around Milwaukee before his reading
how he hit on everything that passed before his eyes.
And his word poems glisten with love dew hope
for all ears on weekends, sunburns.
You two must have led drinks and talk of fun lust
perhaps perusing *Playboy* on the beach.
Now, after the bookstore, I walk horizontal
off to the Haggerty Museum on Marquette's campus
to see the Keith Haring exhibit, his construction
boards you know, the orange babies and dogs
witness from the I-94 freeway ramp, tagged art inside
studios now, what covered the shells
of groundbreaking Jesuit museums. Milwaukee
in the 80s, innocent, unfolding the lives of the poets
and artists suddenly thrust into the eyes and minds of students.
How naïve I was back then, how much you understood.
I find solace in those instructive strolls down
avenues in Midwestern cities and seek thought
bubble blues and greens from channel four morning show
interviewers on videotape asking Haring artful questions.
I know letters are mostly filled with confidence
as I pet the goldfish in the ponds at Mayfair Mall
and throw coins to them and wish for Jack Gilbert
to come visit me in my sleep like some
magical San Francisco and Spicer is there too
holding a drink and reciting a poem.
Each personality glows like minds linked under beams
of light. Write or phone before I arrive next week
and we'll drink whiskey to lost poet
words, club hop in dark nights like it was the 80s again.

Summer 2015

Les Invalides

Wrap me and cremate me
take me from the valley of geraniums
under the willows on St. Helena
by boat and swoop sea to the light of Paris.
Lay me among the cannons and canopy beds
of heaven, symbol wars and empires.
Visit me a thousand times a year
my coffin sculpted from red quartzite
on green marble, unbreakable stone of Gods.
Pray with me and historicize me
baptize me and favorite first communion me.
Tell lies about me, make ornaments of me.
Play games with me while lunching
on tea and biscuits, dessert for the masses
loaves and fishes with me on the sunny
banks of oceans, plant trees of poems for me.
Canonize me and movies of me eternal
delights from me flaming angels brilliant
in old age with the elixir of life from me.
They will all remember me they will all
forget to forget me they will all
saint me a teacher study me
never turning back to me only for
strategy and wonder me, silent eyes of me.

Ode to Hart Crane's Bridge

He imagined a world no one can remember.
His gods formed iron and steel
cement blocks lightly the heart.
His wide eyes gypsy clouds, sudden leaves
cruelty (hope) of nightly daytime shadows.
He looked in the mirror and criticized
himself, not the world. Worlds made him thin
made him want to be the reader and writer
of the poem. The poem was his thought.
It was born of him, built from toppling bricks
shoved slowly, carefully into place.
Modern mind in Cuba the bridge to US.
New York in skyscraper heaven.
Heaven us and embrace the world.
Giant boats, his escape, the platform
the ancient consumes the new.
Born of the last and only century.

Honey Creek Skate Park

Windy day sun and clouds mix afternoon dust
blown into kid's eyes at the skate park.
They practice kick flips grinds slide into one another
like bodies or pavement cracks causing rifts
and/or special feelings. Boys' bodies and girls' bodies
look into the distance, mix each other up in sport open
to diversity, a punk angst and music melting pot.
They accept each other immediately notice how
the skinny girl in green Vans carves better than most boys.
One shy 14 year old, black hoody lifts his courage,
asks for tips from the Queen of asphalt heaven.
How should I raise my board when executing
wood grip ledge kick turn backwards gleam the cube.
Railings edge grab hold spin and land.
He listens, eyes widen, the girl drops the heel flip a
time out and nod owns a precise version
of her, hair raising eyebrow, her pale face, heart lines
drag away from their bodies in a dream.
He dips unsure never mind a board to crash
the bar, his leg bleeds, his pride thrashed. Wind blows
again, cold air, his hair back from his eyes red
filled with tears. He fades into her, falls from handles
like so much first love between social outcasts.
Free blossom form new tricks light as leaves in heavy
wind. They feel the weight of cement blocks,
large love hearts covered over by ripped T-Shirts, dirty jeans
in honey light where youth runs away into each
other with a crash and sudden flame – a little lustful
and painful nonconformity. Together
on boards lovely team up, create and throw a vicious.

Four Dreams

1. AN OLDER DREAM (FOR JEN)

And you asked me to take your arms
in mine help you to the roof for sun

and a hook from your family picture
hurting your hair straightened among

piles of books on the wooden floor
new smoke and laughter rising to the ceiling.

And the stars together made light
of the soft night sky, the price of bodies.

And the windows helped us to think
of rooms in tall college brick buildings

you were self-conscious with age.
Labradors silent on the rug quite old

creaking doors always open to you.
Midwest love like Omaha darling

babies in your eyes – baptismal churches
it was sentences written in the day

brightness from photos on the swings
in the park behind your apartment.

They broke your driver side window
drowned us in heavy glass shards.

Back to dying my dark hair red
we built a whole new universe

together we wanted to be human
people standing, sounds on the beach.

2. A NEWER DREAM (FOR KATY)

Make a joke about music
and it backfires.
"I'm the singer" she says
with a wink, her arms
clutch a portrait of ballerinas.
We swap meet today
as I look for trinkets
and books (of course)
antiques and usable furniture.
I spot an Underdog mask,
red and blue (notice the color)
hanging from a wobbly shelf.
"Try it on" she says
suggesting something
or maybe nothing.
I don't know how
her eyes know at that one
moment, but she does.
So I put down
my vacuum, my wooden
wine box and she wraps
the mask around my face
ties it in the back.
I can't see.
Then she turns me around
and kisses me.
In my dreams
this is what falling
in love feel likes.

3. A Dream Song (for Cyn)

Reading *Portrait* in a bar is better
than in a brothel, but you disagree
and tell me to go to the strip club
in Butternut. "But it is closed," I say
and tell you that I thought
about you last night while looking
for small tattoos for the party.
Later, people arrive with their
own grills and we are confused.
Even more when they take them home
still hot from cooking burgers
and shrimp and corn on the cob.
And Angela is there and Joan too
and we smile at them for what
seems like days until you ask about
my trip to Ireland and how the Irish
must like me and my green eyes.
We stand in black t-shirts with
silhouettes of birds, small sounds
and I think of the tutu and laugh again
with black socks and pink trim.
We are both smart and sexy
and play badminton in the side
yard. I flip the racket under one leg
and ask, "can anyone do that?" You
stop and then laugh so everyone can
hear how funny I am. And I laugh too
until we fall to the ground
laughing and hiding our smiles
from the world. And then you go
and I say goodbye in the night
time stars. It is best for us to go.
But it still makes me sad when I wake.

4. GLORIOUS YEAR DREAM (FOR JENNA)

I am alone in the office.
I ask for a drink and you oblige.
However, when a bartender enters
you don't know what to say.
He stands in silence.
I interview you like a reporter
from the Journal/Sentinel
and count the names of beers
on the wall of a run-down tavern
in Milwaukee where bowling
is played in the basement.
Pins set by hands, not machines.
You remark at how sunny it is
outside and how dark it is inside
and then we start writing furiously
on bar napkins adding characters
and plots with radical Sundays.
The first one we talk about is
Charlie, a ragged clawed poet
as deep as a crevasse, the grand
canyon, a wind blown shack
in the outer territories. Then we
go to UWM and look for the bar
in the basement of the union.
You ask me about Liddy and we
have lunch and I kneel before
you with a Shakespeare play
in my hand. You ask, "Which one?"

A List of Physical Demands
(for a Teaching Job I applied for)

Repetitive movement of hands and fingers.
Typing and/or writing.
Frequent standing and/or sitting.
Occasional walking, stooping, kneeling or crouching.
Reach with hands and arms.
Visually identify, observe and assess.
Talk and hear. The noise level
in the work environment is usually moderate.

What about listening or doing, helping
instructing, advising. No ironic mention of Bartleby?
Apparently, you preferred not to.
Might I inquire…what do I need to stoop for?
Or crouch? Am I being asked to conquer
new regions of the world or perhaps hide
from students, lunge under my desk
in fear of those who will not learn.
Fearful of my student evaluations
after they take a test. Here's a tip;
make students fill out evaluations
on a day when they are happy. I always
find a spring day to be ideal as they will
soon be released into the warm world
and realize how cold it can be. Optimists.
Maybe fools as was I. They need
inspiring teachers and love of learning
magical oyster, freshly from the sea
of life. How it looks and smells funny—
a nugget of truth to swallow.
Therefore, hire away, job market.
We all find it demanding and do what
we can to form the most of our job lives.
A highlight of brief utterances
culled from a lifetime of defining moments.

The Wanderer

Pluto planet PL
plots long and drifty
Greek voyages.
Gods surround space
in our heads, our eyes
form the night sky.
They photograph us
each finger nail
in the celestial playbook.
Tombaugh analyzed
every single negative
from the astrograph
connected dots
in the heavens.
Little movements
a large moon and debate
trajectory accidentally.
Discovery telescope
told the tale
from Mars Hill
in Flagstaff
on planet Percy Lowell
distantly spinning
askew like a teenager
wandering the entire
galaxy in the ancient
orbital path
of a 17 degree
deviation.

We Open Ourselves

We open for seconds, like cameras, see worlds our personal way
take snapshots of classrooms, people who help us decide.
We sing like birds, fly above trees in our sleep ignoring the ground
stay where we build our nests, shiver together in winter.
We are visible and large as oceans unable to displace,
overflow onto land when our emotions cannot hold.
We praise each other and are jealous of those we do not love
worship ideas that will eventually abandon our life desire.
We wander through closets of the past, clothe ourselves
in red velvet and ermine robes, the family the future of thought.
We shape our hair daily and weekly, see our mirrors clearly
in perspective, we hold one another and hands tightly.
We are always around, present in our self-effacing roles
our position languishing underground, ancestors buried beneath rock.
We shape the city and the pastoral, we hold both in our bones
depend on upbringing and bias the television of futures.
We hate our countries and people who inhabit lower depths
and we discipline ourselves after we judge who shall be disciplined.
We talk sweetly and write poems to imaginary poets in spiritland
sunny heaven like magical Iceland smooth moon yellow cameras.
We fear and hex inhuman, stick pins in Voodoo doll ex-lovers
thanksgiving perceived by the small and morbidly instant.
We eat our friends at twilight, crawl vacant with some beauty
innocent at birth, God is a gigantic fist and blind as a bat.
We are Venus and Adonis in our minds, dance when we are able.
We open ourselves yearly, swoop unbound like dreamers.

The Weeds

There is deep down in me something lawless. Always, whether my mind wills it or not,
I find myself on the side not of the weeder but of the weeds.

—STEPHEN MACKENNA, *from his journal, 27 June 1907*

Wander outside comfort zone
in European city states
or South American towns
soak up enlightenment. Notice
oppression and decision, faces
of people shaped like clouds
before the rain. Take the night
sky in the palm of your hand
capture traces of earth
as a present to yourself. Outgrow
feelings and stale relationships.
Wear galoshes to seem out of touch
with reality. Distribute pamphlets
on the streets of Las Vegas.
Squeeze the labor out of every job.
Ask for a raise, weekly
even when el jefe says he
cannot afford more money.
Cover your eyes with glue
and a sleep mask. Run into the street
blame the drivers for swerving.
Cover yourself in blankets
and struggle with your taxes.
You are about to be pulled
from the ground, hair and all.
Make it count!

Poem for Jim Chapson

I wrote a postcard last night and placed it in a frame.
I crawled all the way home after a nightcap at the bar.
You sorted holy cards in your room and swept them under the rug.
You called yourself Tarzan and swung from town to town.
Eric survived the batting practice program and tipped generously.
Paul played the xylophone on his radio program and called it art.
Jeff recorded all of us on camera and pretended it was a wedding.
You were dressed in a white veil and held a bottle of whiskey.
Eamonn kissed the bottle before he offered us a glass.
I told a story that was well received. I recently forgot what
it was about and told the doorman my belief system.
He laughed loudly and stole a kiss from his girlfriend.
She wore a purple dress and sang songs from the lobby.
We all enjoyed a dinner of salmon, capers with red wine reduction.
You prayed that we would all go to heaven, and we did.

Shall I

write about this other poet grand
in our lives who buys me a Hacker
Pschorr wheat (or two) at Blu
on top of the Pfister Hotel down
town MKE and talks of Oppen
at her reading when she was 26
terrified only to recently send back
the wine too sweet taken off her
bill at the request of management
who was told by the University to
treat with kid gloves and delicate
maneuvers?
And the blood moon glows majesty
over us and the cheese plate with
chocolate and drunken strawberries
makes a move to our mouths and
AWP in Washington DC and old
friends and young friends and
friends my age sincere friends
that you can hang with in the base
ment of the Brown Bottle at old
Schlitz Brewery way and scribble
ideas onto a page every day like it
was your job. Forever and ever
writing a book to be released some
where in the future we must feel
inevitable.

Kit Nash's Irish Castle Drinks 1999

Summer forgiveness, light thru windows in a bar:
heaven. Afternoon feels like a firefly's glow
our throats are dry from the day before.
First glass of sunlight. Second glass, third.
We pray with our soft ideas and our hardness too.
James talks with Danny Devine leaning over
wooden railings and strokes the bartender's ego.
Would you like another? I say yes and look
at the pool table, a stain on the edge of the green felt.
Danny says a regular spilled his beer last week and knew
what a mortal sin that was. James says, "We all
know mortal sins and never confess, only venial
ones count." We move along in similar song.
I pray for the day to never end.

Poem for the Penultimate Irish Literature Class

Students don't care for poetry.
You have to trick it into them
with frenzied learning.
They stroll around the tree of life
shoes thrown off
all the livelong day.
Only glances toward the center,
a look instead
of mind touch slouches
towards literature class to be born.
And poetry is about
love, enticing with apple
creation themselves questions
for trust of a serpent like Joyce
writhing around the floor
for his sibling's sake.
We are safely inside
word love and brain theater.
Cultivation over months
competes with business world outside.
Beckett pauses Godot.
His ontological point enlightens
stars sudden in European sky
understanding elusive
as most of the world.
Brains develop slowly realize
me twenty some years
ago sometimes and faster few souls
want to impress.
Many wait silent for hours to pass
tree turns winter quickly
thoughts of more important
classes. Courses that have a point.
My points are pointless points. Clever
maybe, but pointless. And I plead that they
will be able to make smart remarks
or quip at the next party
attended. They laugh
say usual poetry talk rarely outside
of these walls looks

around only to ask
more questions
poetry! what symbols of masters.
We trade dance move
secrets I pride and keen intuition
where hooks knock loudly
on doors questions
with timpani drums made
of gold. Wake the boatman to ferry
them across
river water source.
Until the treeless world again
asks last minute questions or complaints
the amount of sources
for the final paper due soon.
Then, silence. Clean up notes fun
challenge
strong take chances
to learn some
fact to integrate trust someone
who wants passion
to fill learners
still and infuse large glasses.
Word sees/knows
light in all its glorious forms.

Middle Journal

*Sleep to the noise of running water / To-morrow to be crossed, however deep; /
This is no river of the dead or Lethe, / To-night we sleep / On the banks of the
Rubicon – the die is cast; / There will be time to audit / The accounts later,
there will by sunlight later / And the equation will come out at last.*

—LOUIS MacNIECE, *Autumn Journal*

When the filling station seemed empty by the time I arrived
it saddened me to no end and there were times when I burst
out in tears at the sound of the fears in my head, a nervous voice
sparked by a soul in the kitchen or the sewing room with
a purple carpet shedding wool like many sounds I heard, panic
for right choices, deals, the windy words from blustery old
relatives with foolish eyes moving this way and that, not sure
themselves, but blindly confident. It was often misconstrued
often. And I couldn't wage in my head for too long because
I wanted to discover. And even that was stifled on occasion
simple in the hands of the decider as if life had been this way
forever and everyone agreed. And to go against this was utter
craziness since time was tested and true and according to
doctrine, which doctrine they couldn't say, but it was important
weather test right in the great sky of Midwestern America, bustle
of the city, mores of the quiet country, the old muddle of what
runs best for us forever. A fingernail clings to a word or a quiet
child sobbing at the edge of the churchyard wanting to be told
the truth by way of a quiet brook at the back of suburban houses
carrying sound and water on the island like a noon funeral cry.
Summer goes south while my head stays in the same place
never knowing the way, but hearing a line from the paper next
to the painted shed, the sanctum of music and books, the desire
of the sale and someone softly singing like a bird on a window
ledge, the dead leaves underneath to break my fall, my leap
into the abyss of being alone, of wanting to be alone with my
latchkey or combination lock upon my heart and my mind.
The trouble with my youth included silence, unsure of how
to proceed. But also not knowing how to ask, what to say
with silence all around and no one to identify with. Mostly
the other outcasts awkwardly in short lines and me on the cusp
waiting for the right moment and then missing it, often.
But we all learn from these times, the small forgotten days
that have made us into ourselves. People showed me what

I didn't want to become. But people are at heart honest
even when they lie in order to impress. They become each
other in all ways and the side line trips into light where truths
wander over themselves, ready to be plucked like petals
of discovery, petals of lips and red roses small and powerful
journey to change the pulses of girls and boys everywhere.
We have all suffered with strength, the overwhelming
stuff of goods and baggage and many can cry quite emotional
or mesmerized by a new set of arms and legs intertwined
in the night. Our plaudits and aspersions like the sizzle sound
of an ice cube melting fast in hot tea, or a stove with
a grease top flare up, the eternal problems of life mixed gently
among death. Thrust silent in the prisons of pattern home–
bound methods where my plate was white and clean with
noise, the collision of oceans, the new opposite sex, a series
of well-marked stages divided by a small absence of thunderous
lustre attending the midnight sessions, assembly, correspondence
activities for the whisper of envy. Belief is where my childhood
went and adulthood surely pulled in the ways of what faith.
This devotional practice is life among the people, in solitude
out where the confessor stands and asks for a willingness
to suffer with our minds brutalized, by money and for fear
of the conversion of apostates with simplicity and roguery.
A novice at Marquette HS heard me talking heresy one day
and reminded me to think of Christ's dying for the pure love
of us. I remained silent, feared I shall ultimately remain
what I was born. The return to the word, the whippoorwill
in my head repeating the wind, the eternal balance of rights
and wrongs and which way you tend to swing with true advice
the shape of the fold like wrinkled clothes under hot irons.
And the novice also told me a story about going to see
the Rocky Horror Picture Show, the spectacle at midnite
at the Oriental Theater and getting hit on quickly running
out of the bathroom. An eye opening experience, sadly
not a pants opening experience. And who knows of these
incidents, an attempt to try on various hats and oil slickers
even by men devoted to God. The bigger and smaller men
and women, the transgendered, the saved and the damned
the banquet of flesh in comfortable skin and the frontal lobe
develops a little every day. And he who hesitates is lost,
quine risqué rien n'a rein.

I Am Permitted to Return to Ireland in Memory of Youth

Youth eternal, pasture forever turned
up into the starry sky.
Clever my days like school
boys fighting in the fields
about sport, the pitch of minds.
But this place is made to be ever
green, folded into thought.
Tall like swings of backyard trees
from the upper middle west.
It always seemed I died old
in my eighties frightened
by my memories. They take us home
create skulls and shadow
kept inside familiar eyes.
She will be the first one I seek when
I arrive, the flames lit like red
flowers in her hair. I keen her
in pictures and paintings, sculpture
gardens dancing from rock
to stone. I lie on the bed and think
of young dark lapses of the heart.
It is an omen of what is to come
what distant blue of who is
and how will come back into life.

Tree Scene with One Red Cloud

Linus tells me how he likes to color with crayons
but also adds highlights with markers because they
don't hurt his hand as much when he is pushing
hard, making the waxy green stick like wet leaves.
What are crayons made of anyway, he asks, they
last longer than markers and they are smaller,
seem to color more space on the page with blue
in the background. I think it looks like rain
outside and on the page too. I like your tree, I say.
He says, it's going to be a tree-house with
salmon colored butterflies and a silver and brown
stone path. And when I am done I will give it to
mom and to my brother, Holden because they both
like tree-houses. They are symbols for escape, I say.
Linus smiles, responds, I know.

Works Cited

Allen, Donald. Editor. *The New American Poetry: 1945-1960*.
    Berkeley: University of California Press, 1960.

Beckett, Samuel. *Waiting for Godot / En Attendant Godot: A Bilingual Edition*.
    Translated from the original French Text by the Author.
    New York: Grove Press, 1954.

Beroul. *The Romance of Tristan*. Translated by Alan S. Fedrick. New York: Penguin, 1970.

Berryman, John. *His Toy, His Dream, His Rest*. 308 Dream Songs.
    New York: Farrar, Straus and Giroux, 1969.

DuPlessis, Rachel Blau. *Wells*. New York: Montemora Foundation, 1980.

Gilbert, Jack. *Collected Poems*. New York: Knopf, 2014.

Gregory, Horace. *Spirit of Time and Place*. New York: Norton, 1973.

Gregory of Tours. *The History of the Franks*. Translated with an Introduction
    by Lewis Thorpe. New York: Penguin, 1976.

Joyce, James. *Ulysses. The Corrected Text*. New York: Vintage/Random House, 1986.

Liddy, James. *Baudelaire's Bar Flowers*. Santa Barbara: Capra Press/White Rabbit, 1975.

Liddy, James. *Collected Poems*. Omaha: Creighton University Press, 1994.

Liddy, James. *Fest City*. Dublin: Arlen House, 2010.

MacKenna, Stephen. *Journals and Letters*. Edited with a Memoir by E. R. Dodds.
    San Rafael, California: Coracle Press, 2007.

MacNeice, Louis. *Collected Poems*. Edited by Peter McDonald.
    Wake Forest University Press, 2013.

Niedecker, Lorine. *Collected Works*. Jenny Penberthy, Editor.
    Berkeley: University of California Press, 2002.

Noyes, Alfred. Editor. *The Golden Book of Catholic Poetry*. Pennsylvania: Lippincott, 1946.

Oppen, George. *Selected Prose, Daybooks, and Papers*. Edited with an Introduction
    by Stephen Cope. Berkeley: University of California Press, 2007.

Oppen, Mary. *Meaning a Life*. Santa Rosa: Black Sparrow Press, 1976.

Ovid. *The Metamorphoses. Translated and with an Introduction by Horace Gregory*.
    New York: Viking Press, 1958.

Spicer, Jack. *The Collected Books of Jack Spicer*. Edited with Commentary
    by Robin Blaser. Santa Rosa: Black Sparrow Press, 1989.

Weber, Brom. Editor. *The Letters of Hart Crane, 1916-1932*.
    Berkeley: University of California Press, 1965.

Born in Illinois in 1973, TYLER FARRELL received his undergraduate degree at Creighton University, Omaha, Nebraska where he studied with Eamonn Wall. In 2002 he received his doctorate from UW-Milwaukee where he studied with James Liddy. He has published two books with Salmon Poetry: *Tethered to the Earth* (2008), and *The Land of Give and Take* (2012); and has contributed a biographical essay on James Liddy for Liddy's *Selected Poems* (Arlen House, 2011). Farrell is currently a visiting assistant professor at Marquette University, and lives in Madison, Wisconsin, with his wife Joan and their two children. His Morrissey imitations are said to be legendary.

Photograph by Maryam Tunio

www.salmonpoetry.com

"Like the sea-run Steelhead salmon that thrashes upstream to its spawning ground,
then instead of dying, returns to the sea – Salmon Poetry Press
brings precious cargo to both Ireland and America in the poetry it publishes,
then carries that select work to its readership against incalculable odds."

TESS GALLAGHER